BATGIRL

VOLUME

BATGIRL

VOLUME 5
DEADLINE

GAIL SIMONE
MARGUERITE **BENNETT** writers

FERNANDO **PASARIN**
JONATHAN **GLAPION**
ROBERT **GILL** JAVIER **GARRÓN**
MATT **RYAN** artists

BLOND ROMULO **FAJARDO, JR.** colorists

DEZI **SIENTY** ROB **LEIGH** DAVE **SHARPE** letterers

ALEX **GARNER** collection cover artist

BATMAN created by BOB **KANE**

KATIE KUBERT CHRIS CONROY Editors – Original Series
MATT HUMPHREYS DAVE WIELGOSZ Assistant Editors – Original Series ROBIN WILDMAN Editor
ROBBIN BROSTERMAN Design Director – Books ROBBIE BIEDERMAN Publication Design

BOB HARRAS Senior VP – Editor-in-Chief, DC Comics

DIANE NELSON President DAN DIDIO and JIM LEE Co-Publishers GEOFF JOHNS Chief Creative Officer
AMIT DESAI Senior VP – Marketing and Franchise Management
AMY GENKINS Senior VP – Business and Legal Affairs NAIRI GARDINER Senior VP – Finance
JEFF BOISON VP – Publishing Planning MARK CHIARELLO VP – Art Direction and Design
JOHN CUNNINGHAM VP – Marketing TERRI CUNNINGHAM VP – Editorial Administration
LARRY GANEM VP – Talent Relations and Services ALISON GILL Senior VP – Manufacturing and Operations
HANK KANALZ Senior VP – Vertigo and Integrated Publishing JAY KOGAN VP – Business and Legal Affairs, Publishing
JACK MAHAN VP – Business Affairs, Talent NICK NAPOLITANO VP – Manufacturing Administration SUE POHJA VP – Book Sales
FRED RUIZ VP – Manufacturing Operations COURTNEY SIMMONS Senior VP – Publicity BOB WAYNE Senior VP – Sales

BATGIRL VOLUME 5: DEADLINE

DC Comics, 4000 Warner Blvd., Burbank, CA 91522
A Warner Bros. Entertainment Company.
Printed by RR Donnelley, Salem, VA, USA. 4/24/15. First Printing.

ISBN: 978-1-4012-5511-4

Library of Congress Cataloging-in-Publication Data

Simone, Gail, author.
Batgirl. Volume 5 / Gail Simone ; [illustrated by] Fernando Pasarin.
pages cm. — (The New 52!)
ISBN 978-1-4012-5511-4
1. Graphic novels. I. Pasarin, Fernando, illustrator. II. Title.
PN6728.B358S6 2014
741.5'973—dc23
2014011633

Angela Ramirez was the smartest girl in her small Baja town. She knew the Periodic Table at age six.

She wakes up unable to breathe.

Until last week, she was *happy*.

--WGTP AT HALF PAST THE HOUR AND THE WEATHERMAN SAYS WE CAN EXPECT ANOTHER UNSEASONABLE *SCORCHER* TODAY, WITH TEMPS IN THE HIGH 90s...

... YOU KNOW THE WHOLE *CITY'S* GONNA BE SMILING TODAY, SO BE SURE TO WEAR LIGHT CLOTHES AND BRING PLENTY OF SUNSCREEN.

DID SOMEONE FORGET TO TELL MR. SUN THAT IT'S *FEBRUARY?*

Got a job with dozens of people under her.

She was so happy.

I SAY, IF THIS IS GLOBAL WARMING, *BRING IT ON,* AM I RIGHT?

Ms. Ramirez married young but well, and for love. She gave birth to a beautiful daughter.

Until she had what therapists call a *breakthrough.*

She started having dreams, *terrible* dreams. Every single night.

HOT ONE TODAY, MS. RAMIREZ. GOOD FOR *BUSINESS,* RIGHT?

SURE IS, TODD.

SO THIS IS SMILIN' STEVE AT *WGTP* SAYING, WHY NOT MAKE TODAY "WEAR YOUR SWIMSUIT TO WORK DAY"?

NO FILMING ALLOWED. TASTY TREATS WITHIN!

Gotham is a city of the day.

But increasingly, Angela sees only *night.*

I admit it-- sometimes I hate the morning.

BARBARA, IF YOU DON'T GET UP, I'M GIVING YOUR BREAKFAST TO THE *CAT.*

MFMF... ...COUPLE MORE HOURS...

FINE. CAT GETS THE BACON, THEN.

BACON?

And here I thought life couldn't *get* any better.

DON'T YOU *DARE,* DAD! THAT CAT IS *ALREADY* A FREAKING *WHALE.*

CLEAN PANTS, CLEAN PANTS, CLEAN PANTS.

Sleeping in and bacon.

My needs are few.

COMING. I'M COM-ING.

SORRY, ALASKA.

BUT YOU *ARE* GETTING *HUGE.*

Have to eat quick and fly.

Got things to *do* this morning, and have a Master's exam in the afternoon.

I mean, I could *skip* breakfast. It's no big deal, just...

...I don't know. I want to stay.

It's corny. I don't deny it.

GOOD MORNING, SUNSHINE!

But there's just something about breakfast with my dad.

We're kind of inseparable.

UH, I DON'T REMEMBER SAYING "WHOA," THERE, HOSS.

KEEP THE SWINE TRAIN COMIN'.

WHERE'RE MOM AND JAMES, JR.?

It's precious...

...my school, my boyfriend, my friends, my beautiful family.

YOUR MOTHER'S GONE SHOPPING, SHE SAID TO WISH YOU LUCK ON YOUR EXAM.

YOUR BROTHER'S HELPING AT THE HOMELESS SHELTER, BLESS HIS HEART.

So many have nothing, and I have so much.

Makes me overwhelmed, sometimes.

HEY, SWEETIE... YOU OKAY?

I'M FINE, DAD.

REALLY, I AM.

I have my family.

And I feel like my smile will last forever.

I LOVE YOU, SWEETHEART.

FM FOO TOOF.

I HAVE TO RUN. DUTY CALLS.

WHAT ARE YOU UP TO, TODAY, BABS?

OH, I THOUGHT I'D HANG AROUND WITH CHARISE. MEET UP WITH RICKY LATER TONIGHT FOR A JOG, MAYBE.

WELL, PERFECT WEATHER FOR IT.

IT'S A BEAUTIFUL DAY.

It is.

Every day is a beautiful day...

By the doofiest person I know.

NICE, CLUMSY, BUT NICE.

Charise Carnes.

Also known as Daybreak.

We met trying to rescue the same couple from a downed power line.

Now we try to help people, where we can, together.

THAT HURT.

YOU SUCK AS A BEST FRIEND, BLUEBELLE.

Okay, she's a bit spoiled.

Her dad's one of the richest men in the city, and he...

...well, he indulges her. Whatever she wants.

But I can't help it, I dearly love this goofball.

We'd climb to the moon for each other.

IT'S TOO HOT FOR SURPRISE SPARRING, PARTNER.

I WAS JUST GOING TO SAY.

HEY, WHAT IS THAT?

IT'S "ODE TO JOY," FROM BEETHOVEN'S NINTH SYMPHONY.

DID THEY TEACH YOU NOTHING AT BOARDING SCHOOL?

"IT'S NOT THE MUSIC I CARE ABOUT, BLUEBELLE.

"IT'S THE SUGAR AND CHOCOLATE."

MAKE THE *CALL*, DAYBREAK.

THEN STOP THE *TRUCKS* ANY WAY YOU *CAN!*

HEY! THAT'S *JOEY'S* BIKE! SHE'S TAKING JOEY'S *BIKE!*

*Ode to Joy.
It was a poem,
first. German.*

*It was a call to
brotherhood.*

*.What kind of sick
mind would do
this? In Gotham?*

Children.

*Someone's
got to be
targeting
children.*

DON'T
EAT
THAT!

HEY, DAMMIT. DON'T YOU *PUT* THAT *THING IN YOUR MOUTH!*

HEY, WHAT THE *HELL*, LADY?

OKAY. I KNOW YOU'RE SURPRISED. SO I'M NOT TAKING THIS *PERSON-ALLY.*

SIMMONS. I KNOW THIS AIN'T IDEAL OR NOTHIN'.

BUT IF SHE TRIES TO GIVE THOSE KIDS THAT STUFF...

...YOU TAKE THAT SHOT.

COPY THAT, LIEUTENANT BULLOCK.

GOD HELP US ALL.

HEY, COP.

WHAT?

HEADS UP.

This "Mother Mercy" has already killed.

She'll poison those kids and then herself, I know it.

The suicide rate in Gotham has been unusually high, lately.

Nobody seems to know why.

I'M ARRESTED, AREN'T I?

GEE.

LET ME *THINK*.

IT'S TIME, LITTLE ANGELS.

COME TO MOTHER.

...*REPEAT*, BLUEBELLE HAS CROSSED ON SCENE, SIMMONS. IF SHE GETS IN THE WAY...

...TAKE HER *OUT*, YOU *HEAR* ME?!

COPY THAT.

NO.

YOU CAN'T MAKE US DO THIS.

OH YES, I CAN, DARLING.

--NE.

NOT ALONE.

That's when I decided I was going to put this day away and forget it ever happened.

The children were saved, that's what I cling to.

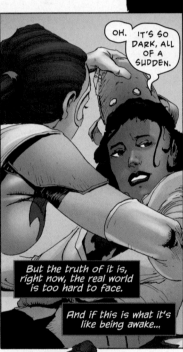

OH. IT'S SO DARK, ALL OF A SUDDEN.

But the truth of it is, right now, the real world is too hard to face.

And if this is what it's like being awake...

MY FAMILY.

I CAN SEE THEM.

AND THEY'RE SMILING.

...I would rather be *dreaming*.

SILVER

GAIL SIMONE writer **FERNANDO PASARIN** penciller **JONATHAN GLAPION** inker **BLOND** colorist **ALEX GARNER** cover artist

GOTHAM CITY...

I'm being tailed.

And whoever they are, they're good.

Since I caught those repulsive Brisby Killers a few months ago, there have been at least three copycat groups.

The original killers have quite the little fan following, even while they rot in prison.

Bored college kids wearing Halloween masks, committing home invasions.

Tail or no... got a good lead on one of these new ones.

Put them down hard enough, maybe other copycats might think twice.

OH, THERE YOU ARE, YOU BASTARDS. YOU LIKE BREAKING INTO PEOPLE'S HOMES AND TERRORIZING THEM, RIGHT?

TONIGHT, YOU LEARN WHAT TERROR IS.

OH.

STRIX, I KNOW GOTHAM COPS DON'T HAVE THE BEST REPUTATION, BUT THEY ARE ACTUALLY *REALLY* GOOD AT RECOVERING LOST KIDS.

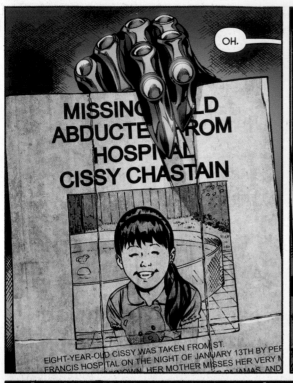

MISSING CHILD ABDUCTED FROM HOSPITAL CISSY CHASTAIN

EIGHT-YEAR-OLD CISSY WAS TAKEN FROM ST. FRANCIS HOSPITAL ON THE NIGHT OF JANUARY 13TH BY PER... UNKNOWN. HER MOTHER MISSES HER VERY M... ...PAJAMAS. AND...

TAP TAP TAP

YOU WANT *ME* TO FIND HER. WHY IS THIS SO IMPORTANT TO YOU?

DUE TO A FEVER IN HER INFANCY, CISSY IS UNABLE TO SPEAK. PLEASE HELP US BRING HER HOME. CALL: 555-1887.

TAP TAP TAP

OH. OH, HONEY.

I'VE SPOTTED ONE, MISS TARGA. *TWO*, ACTUALLY.

THEY SEEM TO BE *FEEDING*.

THE *DEVILS*.

SHALL WE ENGAGE THEM, SIR?

NO, IT'S TOO LATE FOR THAT LOT. THEY'RE LOST.

AND THE TWO WILL BE STRONGEST NOW. WE WAIT.

I've already called G.C.P.D. to pick up the copycats.

It's this second phone call I'm dreading...

BZZT!

YES, YOU'VE REACHED *CHARISE CARNES*, HOW MAY I HELP YOU?

I hate doing this. I hate it.

Her damn **goons** just tried to kill my dad.

But **no one** has her connections to the underworld in Cherry Hill.

MS. CARNES, OR **KNIGHTFALL**, IF YOU PREFER. YOU KNOW MY VOICE.

I KNOW IN SOME DEEP PART OF YOUR **TWISTED** SOUL, YOU THINK YOU'RE **PROTECTING** GOTHAM.

TRUTHFULLY, **BATGIRL?** I'VE ALWAYS FELT WE WERE ON THE SAME **SIDE**.

WE'RE **NOT**. BE QUIET AND **LISTEN**.

THERE'S A SICK EIGHT-YEAR-OLD GIRL, AND SHE'S BEEN **ABDUCTED**.

CISSY CHASTAIN. I NEED YOU TO PUT THE WORD OUT. HELP ME **FIND** HER.

AND IF I DO THIS GOOD, DECENT THING? WHAT THEN?

YOU **KNOW** WHAT, CHARISE. I WILL **OWE** YOU.

THIS ONE'S **COMPLIMENTARY**. CALL BACK IN TWO HOURS.

I WILL DO EVERYTHING IN MY POWER TO FIND THIS CHILD.

AND BATGIRL...

...GOOD LUCK. *KHICK*

Kind of **sucks** when the person you hate most in the world has the network you can't do **without**.

ALL RIGHT, STRIX.

WE'RE GOING **UNDERCOVER**.

OH. GOD. OW.

AH. IT'S WAKING UP, MISS TARGA.

UNFORTUNATE.

WHAT? WHAT HAPPENED?

YOU'VE BEEN *INFECTED,* I'M AFRAID.

NOTHING TO BE DONE AT THIS POINT.

SOME OF YOU ARE ALREADY *TURNED,* I'M SORRY TO SAY. THE BRIEFCASE, MISS TARGA.

WAIT. WHAT?

NO...

...NO! NO!

YOU'RE *CRAZY!*

DON'T DO THIS!

HUSH, CHILD.

CISSY CHASTAIN'S HOUSE...

OKAY, JUST LET *ME* DO THE TAL--

UGH. SORRY. FORGOT.

It's amazing what you can do with a badge you "found" in the G.C.P.D. ladies' locker room.

MRS. CHASTAIN? I'M SORRY TO BOTHER YOU. I'M DETECTIVE ELLIDGE, AND THIS IS MY SUPERVISOR, DETECTIVE MANNING.

WE KNOW YOU'VE BEEN THROUGH A LOT, BUT CAN WE SPEAK TO YOU AGAIN ABOUT YOUR DAUGHTER, CISSY?

Oh.

What's she's going through... I can't...

...this must have been what Dad went through when I was shot.

OKAY. IT'S OKAY.

And then it all just pours out...no blood at the scene, no ransom demands.

But not much of a trail left, either. Professionals.

But why this girl?

YOU GUYS SAID YOU THINK SHE'LL JUST *TURN UP* OR SOMETHING.

BUT SHE'S JUST A *CHILD*.

I HAVE NO IDEA WHAT YOU'RE *TALKING* ABOUT!

DON'T YOU? THE *BATS* WHO *RUN* THIS CITY, WHO ARE GIVEN *FREE REIN* BY THE *POLICE?*

WHO OWN EVERYTHING FROM THE *SKY* TO THE *SEWERS* THAT CARRY OUR *WASTE?*

Who is this guy?

And how does he know all this?

AND WHO KEEP THE CITY IN *CONSTANT* ECONOMIC TURMOIL, SO THAT NO ONE CAN *LEAVE,* BUT SIMPLY REMAIN FOR THE *SLAUGHTER?*

WAIT. *WHO* DO YOU THINK I'M WITH THERE, SPORT?

WITH *THEM.* THE *BATS.*

THE *VAMPIRES!*

Vampires. He thinks we're all...

...huh.

It does make a weird kind of sense when you think about it.

WE DON'T HAVE *TIME* FOR THIS.

DO LET US KNOW IF WE START TO SPARKLE, YEAH?

DON'T WALK *AWAY* FROM ME, BLOODSUCKER!

I'VE KILLED *DOZENS* LIKE YOU!

OH, SO *THAT'S* HOW IT IS.

FINALLY. SOMEONE TO *CHALLENGE* ME.

Now, Barbara Gordon shouldn't be doing this out on the street.

But Detective Ellidge, well...

...she's a bit of a *discipline* problem.

NGGG.

It *can't be a* coincidence that a man with a vampire obsession shows up at this house, on *this* night, can it?

YOU AND YOUR KIND HAVE BLINDED THE HERD LONG *ENOUGH,* CREATURE!

There's a *connection* here. Got to be.

Just need to calm his *determination,* here.

I hate it when the bad guys plan ahead.

THIS IS THE GOTHAM CITY POLICE.

YOU WILL *DROP YOUR WEAPONS* OR WE WILL OPEN FIRE!

Oh, no.

The *timing.*

Uh, oh.

He's wearing a cup.

A CONSPIRACY OF BATS
GAIL SIMONE writer FERNANDO PASARIN penciller JONATHAN GLAPION inker BLOND colorist ALEX GARNER cover artist

THR--

WAIT!

WAIT. THERE'S NO NEED FOR THIS, GENTLEMEN.

What?

OBSERVE.

What in the hell is Silver up to?

LOWER YOUR WEAPONS, PLEASE, OFFICERS.

I'M A DESPERATE MAN WITH NOTHING TO LOSE, ET CETERA, ET CETERA.

Really?

Is this a suicide-by-cop thing?

PITY.

He's not going to do it, is he?

He won't do it.

WE'RE NOT LOWERING OUR GUNS, BUDDY!

Uh, oh.

KLI-KLAK

GET *DOWN!* EVERY-BODY, TAKE *COVER!*

BUDDA BUDDA BUDDA

Can't let this *happen.*

Even if it blows my cover.

OKAY. GLOVES *OFF,* THEN.

OPEN THIS *DOOR,* DAMN YOU!

BUDDA BUDDA BUDDA

WHAT? NO. THEY'RE GETTING *AWAY!*

And then hot guy's hot assistant shoots me a certain filthy *hand gesture* on the way out.

OKAY.

BUT WE'RE NOT DONE, GUYS.

BE *SEEING* YOU!

MMF!

The only good thing about a creep with a machine gun?

Cops tend to forget the unarmed girls exist for a bit.

But Strix was right...

...too much firepower on the gameboard.

I GOT A BROTHER, USED TO BE G.C.P.D., DID I EVER TELL YOU THAT? HE MOVED TO DETROIT. FOR THE *QUIET.*

LATER...

OKAY, *CHARISE*. I *OWE* YOU FOR THIS INFORMATION.

WE HAD THE PERPS IN OUR SIGHTS, BUT WE LOST 'EM. COPS GOT IN THE WAY.

I KNOW THE FEELING, *BATGIRL*.

AND AS I SAID, THIS ONE'S ON THE *HOUSE*.

FIND CISSY CHASTAIN. BRING THAT LITTLE GIRL *HOME*, PLEASE.

If I had an "archenemy," it'd be this woman-- *Knightfall.*

Shows how *desperate* I am that I'd use *her* contacts.

OKAY, HER TRACKING CAME THROUGH. THE CAR'S AT THE HOME OF A GUY NAMED *UCHIDA*.

SAD FAMILY HISTORY, I MUST SAY.

IF GIRL IS HURT. I KILL. DO NOT TRY TO STOP.

SWEETIE, I KNOW HOW YOU FEEL.

BUT WE'RE NOT *KILLING* ANYONE. I'VE SEEN ENOUGH OF THAT.

PROMISE ME. OR I GO ALONE.

This girl we're trying to find, Cissy Chastain. She's only eight years old...and she's unable to speak, like Mary, here.

She's taking this kidnapping *hard.*

PROMISE ME, MARY.

OUTSKIRTS OF GOTHAM...

THAT WAS RATHER A GRAND, DRAMATIC *GAMBIT*, WOULDN'T YOU SAY, *MISS TARGA?*

A DANGEROUS ONE, MASTER. YOU JUST *NICKED* THE BLOOD VESSELS AROUND THE THYROID GLAND. MASTERFUL.

A BABY'S BREATH DEEPER AND YOU WOULD NEVER HAVE MADE IT HOME.

I CAN'T *LOSE* YOU, MR. UCHIDA.

OH... WELL...

...THIS IS AWKWARD.

I'LL NEED ATTIRE, MISS TARGA. NOW THAT WE'VE ENGAGED THE VAMPIRES, THEY'LL USE THEIR UNGODLY POWERS TO HUNT US.

... OF COURSE, SIR.

YOU'LL NEED YOUR DRINK, SILVER.

ALL OF IT, PLEASE.

I HEARD THE CHILD CRYING, SIR. ARE YOU *CERTAIN* THAT--

IT'S NOT A *CHILD*, DEAR FRIEND.

THAT'S WHAT IT *WANTS* YOU TO BELIEVE.

IT'S A DEMON LORD... A BLOODSUCKING *KILLER*.

FOR YEARS NOW, THIS CITY HAS BEEN UNDER THE CREPE BOOT-HEEL OF THE NIGHTBREED, THE VAMPIRE LORDS AND LADIES WHO MAKE US THEIR *CATTLE*.

YES, MASTER.

AND THEY TAKE THEIR ORDERS FROM ONE WHO DOESN'T EVEN *HIDE* WHAT HE IS, WHO PROUDLY *CALLS* HIMSELF A *BAT*.

AND HE HAS HIS *CONCUBINES*, WOMEN AND GIRLS AND BOYS WHO *ALSO* WEAR HIS FILTHY SIGIL. AND *THRALLS* IN EVERY SEAT OF POWER!

YES, MASTER.

"I WAS *FIFTEEN* WHEN THEY TOOK MY MOTHER. THEY FEARED HER STRENGTH, HER *GOODNESS*.

"I FOUND HER, *DRAINED OF BLOOD*, ALREADY COLD TO THE TOUCH."

I WILL *DESTROY* THEIR KIND, DEAR TARGA.

STARTING WITH *THIS* ONE.

HELLO, DEMON. CRY ALL YOU LIKE. IT'S EXACTLY WHAT WE *WANT* YOU TO DO.

IT WILL ONLY BRING YOUR KIN HERE MORE *QUICKLY*.

Ah. THEY'RE HERE. I *FEEL* IT.

Urgh.

Four messages from Ricky, whom I haven't visited in *days*.

Sorry, Ricky. I'll call you tomorrow, I promise.

KRAC KOOMM

Strix moves like she *knows* where the cameras are.

The Court of Owls are a big sack of losers, but they know how to build an *assassin*.

SHALL I TURN ON ALL THE SECURITY MEASURES, MASTER?

NO...

OKAY...

...WEIRD, RIGHT?

My brother and I never missed a bad horror movie.

I know an open door is bad news.

...LET'S BE GRACIOUS HOSTS AND INVITE THEM *IN*, DEAR TARGA.

BY ALL MEANS.

COME HAVE A *TASTE*, WHY DON'T YOU?

LISTEN, I DON'T KNOW WHAT YOU--

WE'RE NOT *VAMPIRES*, ALL RIGHT?

WE JUST WANT THE *GIRL*.

Uh, oh.

I forgot.

Strix doesn't negotiate.

But we need to know where the girl is.

FLK

FLK

$#%K

Holy crap.

He tagged her.

No one tags her!

Oh.

That hurt...

>GUGH<

After that sp[i] down the stair[s] can barely even see straight.

KLANG

She's going to kill him. Promise or no promise.

Strix's going to take his *head!*

STRIX. LET GO.

UNH!

STOP IT!

YOU...YOU GAVE ME NO *CHOICE.*

AND **YOU**. SIT THE HELL **DOWN**.

GNNNN.

OKAY. IF I HELP YOU UP, YOU'RE NOT GOING TO KILL ME, RIGHT?

Huh. She shrugs.

Don't know if that's a warning or a weird attempt at a joke.

YOU SHOWED ME... **MERCY**.

WE'RE NOT **VAMPIRES**, MR. UCHIDA.

BUT... BUT MY **MOTHER**.

I READ THE G.C.P.D.'S FORENSIC FILES. YOUR MOTHER COMMITTED SUICIDE IN HER BATHTUB, SILVER.

THERE WAS NO BLOOD BECAUSE IT WENT DOWN THE **DRAIN**.

I know he's a kidnapper. I know he's deluded.

But to lose your mother that way...

I'M SORRY. THERE **ARE** NO VAMPIRES.

HELLO? CAN I GO HOME NOW?

Oh, thank God. She's alive.

CISSY...?

HOLY WATER, MR. BENNETT. OUR BLOOD IS *TOXIC* TO YOUR KIND.

WELL. HOW *NOVEL.*

YOU SURPRISE ME, MR. UCHIDA. WE'LL MEET AGAIN.

I GUARANTEE *THAT.*

I...I'm out of my league, here.

What do I tell Cissy's mother?

What do I do with the hot guy and his danger lady? Wait, where--?

--and ironically, *they* just pulled a Batman.

GONE.

OKAY, STRIX...IT'S AGREED, RIGHT?

FROM NOW ON, WE *DON'T* FIGHT THE *UNDEAD.*

AGREED.

And now the *big* question.

How do I convince myself this actually *happened* in the morning?

THE MIDNIGHT MAN

MARGUERITE BENNETT writer **ROBERT GILL** artist **ROMULO FAJARDO, JR.** colorist
CLAY MANN & PAUL MOUNTS cover artists

"...WOULD'VE BEEN A GOOD STORY."

Dick used to *laugh* at me for watching horror movies.

(Dick used to do a *lot* of things, but now he's *gone*, isn't he--)

--"Why do you *watch* this stuff, Babs?" he'd ask. "Gonna give *yourself* nightmares--"

--(No, don't think about that, about him, not now)--

--"I know it does," I'd tell him. "I know I shouldn't."

"But there's the *thrill*."

And that, I think, he understood.

Wait, what was *that*?

The EMF reader is going *haywire*, geez--

--*lethal* amounts of energy.

Normally I don't hear anything from the EMF--

--not because there isn't anything *paranormal* in Gotham--

--not for *Silver*, not for *Andrew Bennett*--

--but because there's just too *much* freakiness going on at *once*.

Spike like *this*, though...

...hmm...the EMF leads me to a house as quiet as the dead...

...usually I wouldn't go into a private home, but something tells me there's more to this story...

...what would *Dick* have done?

HELLO?

Dick laughs so much...

"...laugh at the dark or become part of it," he says.

(He laughed, he said, I mean. Past tense.)

Damian getting killed, and now Dick...

...(Don't think of them, the Robins)--

--Dick used to tease the hell out of me--

--(Was there any other way Dick could tease?)

How I was their misfit, their bat in a flock of birds.

It never bothered me that I wasn't a Robin like Dick and Jason, Tim and Damian...

...I had a different flight, different wings.

CREEEEEK

We were watching some horror movie at Wayne Manor one night--

--Dick knew I loved horror movies.

Dick watched them with me even though he jumped out of his skin.

He always told the same stupid joke--

Bruce taught us the rules of *survival* from every realm he knew.

BATGIRL! YOU'VE GOT TO *HELP* US, WE--

WE--WE USED THE *POEM* AND SUMMONED *THE MIDNIGHT MAN!*

POEM?! OH, NO...

You can fracture a kneecap with 6.92 KN of pressure.

A bullet from a .357 magnum travels at 990 miles per hour.

And when dealing with foul spirits--

--sage is poison.

I attack him, I lose.

I run, I lose.

I stay still, he slurps my spine out, I lose.

My...my face...

...he's... mimicking me...

...you don't get to have my *face.*

You don't get to have my *wings.*

Every kid in Gotham knows the poem about the *Midnight Man.*

Sure as you know the rules for *Bloody Mary,* and the legend of the *Dark Knight.*

A scary story. An urban legend.

A game that children play.

WHAT'S *REAL* AND *UNREAL* AND *SURREAL* BLENDS TOGETHER REALLY *QUICKLY* IN THIS BUSINESS, GUYS.

It wasn't just the training and the rules, for me.

Some nights... the manor was popcorn and movies, too.

But to be a *Robin*...with all that entailed?

I was happier to be a bat in a shelter of my own wings and cave...

...than a robin in a nest of down and thorns.

I DON'T UNDERSTAND-- WHERE DID THE MIDNIGHT MAN *COME* FROM? WHAT DOES HE *WANT?*

I DON'T KNOW...AND I'M NOT WILD ABOUT FINDING OUT...

...I *THINK* HE'S TAKING ON THE SHAPES OF WHAT HE FINDS...

...HE TRIED TO TAKE ON MY *FACE*... I THINK HE'S A *MIMIC*...

...KIND OF LIKE THAT!

Oh, God, that is gross.

Bugs. He's discovered bugs.

How do I beat this thing?

And what comes back to normal?

...but Dick as he teased me, Dick as he laughed...

...(Don't think of him.)

...but I take a terrible risk.

I do think of him.

And it hurts to think of him.

My plan has fallen apart, but I've gotta protect my flock, birds or bats or reckless kids--

--even if I can't fly.

AAGGHH!

SKREEEEEE!

We've got to survive.

I know sage is poison to evil spirits--

--and I know that in horror movies--

The poem that comes back to me, is not about *you*, you faceless creep.

This story isn't yours.

The story was ours--Dick's, Robin's, and mine...

..."Robin redbreast in a cage..."

"...puts all heaven in a rage..."

But I never was a robin.

And heaven can keep its rage.

I have a power all my own...

...Dick Grayson...

...I miss you so damn much.

That was easy. That was *too* easy.

There are rules. This is *wrong*.

Too many unanswered questions.

But they're alive.

I CAN SEE OUTSIDE--

THE LIGHTS FROM THE STREET-LAMPS--

DO ME A FAVOR AND STICK TO *SPIN THE BOTTLE.*

NO ONE PLAYS SPIN THE BOTTLE ANYMORE.

WELL, FINE, STICK TO *MARIO-KART.*

DAMN BLUE SHELLS.

You survived your horror movie, guys.

You survived your game, your urban legend.

Not all of us do.

WHAT IS IT?

CAN YOU *SMELL* THAT?

YUCK--

IT'S LIKE SOME-BODY MIXED IN *BOOZE* AND...WHAT, *CHALK?* AND THESE LITTLE *FLOWER BITS*--

WHY WOULD SOMEONE PUT THAT *CRAP* IN OUR BARRELS?

DO WE NEED TO LOAD IN NEW PAINT?

TOO LATE. WE'VE ALREADY USED IT TO PAINT THE LINES FROM FRANKLIN TO WEST BROAD, AND DOWN OVER ON KIMBALL, TOO.

WEIRD, BUT IT'S ALL RIGHT. NO ONE WILL NOTICE ONCE IT *DRIES*.

"ALL THAT *JUNK* MIXED IN THE BARREL. IT AIN'T WORTH MENTIONING. SOMEONE JUST LOOKING FOR A *THRILL*."

WHEN PAMELA GETS BLUE

GAIL SIMONE writer ROBERT GILL JAVIER GARRÓN artists ROMULO FAJARDO, JR. colorist
CLAY MANN & PAUL MOUNTS cover artists

And that's us: the one and only *Birds of Prey*.

Kind of like the *Justice League*, but with fewer high collars and ten times the *chaos*.

MR. TUCKER-- YOU'RE NO TERRORIST.

YOU'RE *HEALTHY.*

YOU COULD *NEVER* UNDERSTAND.

WHAT IS IT THAT RAIN *HAS* ON YOU?

Mister, you have no idea.

I'M TRULY SORRY.

SNAAP

What the hell?

My Bat-line is hybrid-fiber filament, it could hold a rhino.

JUST GIVE US AN *ADDRESS.*

YOU DON'T BELONG HERE.

I BELONG WHERE HE TELLS ME TO BE!

FOR WHATEVER REASON, *STARLING,* THE CANARY EXPLICITLY SAID NO *KILLING.*

CHICK'S NO FUN ANYMORE, *KATANA.*

Dinah had good intel. Great intel.

How did we not know these guys cou crush bricks?

THREE MONTHS LATER...

Oh.

Oh, *man* it's hot.

It's *godawful* hot.

Second straight week of record-breaking scorchery.

And after three months of looking, I still haven't got a job (or a boyfriend, or even a *potentially* potential boyfriend)...

HEY. HEY, *DAYDREAM GIRL!*

...so I somehow agreed to work in the *dirt* on a lovely Saturday when I *could* be home watching TV, sleeping and eating pancakes.

LOOK AT THESE TOMATOES, HOLY COW!

WE *DID* THIS, YOU KNOW. WE TOTALLY MADE THIS HAPPEN.

RIGHT HERE IN *CHERRY HILL*, NO LESS.

I'll say this about my ever-chipper roomie...she's ridiculously *persuasive.*

HEY, GORDON.

TOMATOES, REMEMBER? WHAT *ARE* YOU LOOKING AT?

NOTHING, ALYSIA.

YOU SHOULD PROBABLY GET A SECURITY CAM.

Past midnight.

Still hot as the hottest *hot*.

I swear, I'm actually thinking of fighting crime in a tank top and jorts.

I have a memory of a friend from college, a hiker who spent her summers in Montana.

She said if you walked two hundred yards off the road, you could be in a place where the civilized world didn't really *exist* anymore.

Even Gotham has bits like that, just to the north, on the mainland of Kane County.

There's nothing but a security gate and some "No Trespassing" signs keeping this compound isolated.

Unseen and unnoticed.

First solid location lead I've *had* on Mr. Rain's op since the lab operation.

Why does a bio-researcher need a militia-style compound?

I KNOW YOU'RE *BEHIND* ME, IVY.

Gotta be this place. It's spooking me.

Or maybe I'm just getting paranoid.

I admit, I've been avoiding coming here to see him.

But he says he *has* to talk to me.

BARBARA! THANK YOU FOR COMING.

GOOD TO...MFF...SEE YOU, *MS. GUTIERREZ.*

I feel awful. I wouldn't blame him if he was calling me here to *dump* me. Heh.

Oh, man. What if he's calling me here to *dump* me?

HE'LL BE *SO* GLAD TO SEE YOU.

I MADE YOU THESE TAMALES...I KNOW YOU LIKE THEM, AND YOU'RE GETTING SO *SKINNY,* BARBARA.

WELL. SINCE YOU *INSIST.*

One thing Ms. Gutierrez and my mom have in common...they turn food into an antidote.

For pretty much *anything.*

I'M... SORRY I'VE BEEN *AWAY...*

GO *IN,* GO *IN.*

305 306

He looks good. He looks...like Ricky.

Urgh. I really *am* a terrible girlfriend.

RICKY...?

I have no idea what to say.

UPTOWN!

YOU OKAY? I *MISSED* YOU.

YEAH. I'M GOOD.

NOW.

He nearly died and he's asking if I'm okay.

HEY, WHY ARE YOU CRYING?

I HAVE NO IDEA.

HAPPY, I GUESS.

... HOPE YOU STAY THAT WAY, BARBARA.

I HAVE SOMETHING TO TELL YOU, AND IT'S HARD.

He is dumping me!

Barbara, for God's sake, get a grip.

RICKY, I KNOW WE DON'T REALLY ACTUALLY LEGITIMATELY EVEN KIND OF DON'T *KNOW* EACH OTHER THAT WELL.

BUT YOU *CAN* TALK TO ME.

A *LAWYER* CAME TO SEE ME, BARBARA. A GOOD ONE.

I'M *SUING* YOUR FATHER.

HE SHOT ME WITHOUT *CAUSE*, AND I'M SUING HIM.

YOU...

WAIT... *WHAT?!*

I-I HAVE TO GO.

BARBARA, LET ME *EXPLAIN*--

I HAVE TO GO.

WELL... *THAT* WENT WELL.

MEANWHILE...

PLEASE...

CANT BREATHE...

WELL, I AM TERRIBLY SORRY, DARLING, BUT THAT'S THE POINT.

*

YES, I KNOW OUR EMPLOYER SAID NO WITNESSES...

I WILL. YES. OF COURSE. JUST TWO LEFT. TALK SOON.

GIVE MY LOVE TO YOUR WIVES.

BzZZZzT
BzZZZzT

ALYSIA?

BARBARA!

I DIDN'T KNOW WHO TO CALL.

ALYSIA, WHAT'S GOING ON? WHERE ARE YOU?

WE'RE AT THE CARTER RESNIK FOUNDATION BUILDING. I TOLD YOU ABOUT THEM, REMEMBER? BIO-RESEARCH?

THEY DO TERRIBLE THINGS, BARBARA.

WE...WE GOT RECRUITED. TO MESS UP THEIR OFFICES.

ALYSIA, CALL THE COPS. BEING ARRESTED IS BETTER THAN BEING DEAD.

ONLY, SOMEONE TIPPED THEM OFF. THEY'VE GOT A KILLER HERE!

Her new friends from the Three Towers organization. I knew something was up, but not this.

WE TRIED. THEY DON'T BELIEVE US!

AND THEY'D NEVER GET HERE IN TIME! I JUST...I JUST...

...I JUST THOUGHT... IF WE DON'T MAKE IT...

COULD YOU CALL MY FAMILY? TELL THEM I LOVE THEM?

WHAT FLOOR ARE YOU ON?

WHAT?

WHAT FLOOR?

"AND LEAVE YOUR PHONE ON, OKAY?

"I CAN GET HOLD OF SOMEONE WHO CAN *HELP*."

My roommate's activism never rose above protests and petty vandalism before.

She must've been talked into this. I'm too terrified to be as *furious* at her as I should be, dammit.

And she picked the *worst* possible target.

It's a dummy corporation run by Mr. Rain, whom Poison Ivy and I dealt with a while back.

He's left *many* disappeared journalists and protestors in his wake.

But not Alysia.

No damn way.

...JUST SAYING THAT ALL THE HARD WORK AND DEDICATION YOU FOUR HAVE SHOWN...WELL, IT'S ABOVE AND *BEYOND.*

YOU'VE BEEN NOTICED. I WAS JUST WONDERING...

...HOW DEDICATED *ARE* YOU, EXACTLY?

LOOK, *MICHAEL,* WE KNOW HOW BAD CARTER RESNIK IS.

WHAT DO YOU WANT *US* TO DO ABOUT IT?

JUST *THIS.*

THIS IS, ESSENTIALLY, THE WORLD'S MOST POWERFUL *STINK BOMB,* MY FRIENDS. MY OWN DESIGN.

A CORRUPT CORPORATION WANTS TO *POLLUTE* OUR CITY? *POISON* OUR CITIZENS?

THIS WILL MAKE THEIR HEADQUARTERS UNINHABITABLE FOR A *WEEK.*

WELL. I CAN'T GIVE NAMES. WE'RE NOT AFFILIATED WITH THREE TOWERS, THOUGH. NOT AT ALL.

LET'S JUST SAY IT'S FOR THE *PEOPLE OF GOTHAM.*

CAREFUL, MS. YEOH.

YOU DON'T WANT TO *OPEN* THAT.

WHO ARE WE DOING THIS FOR?

NEVER MIND, A JOB IS A JOB, I USUALLY SAY.

NO!

GET AWAY FROM ME!

FSSST

AUGSSSSS!

THAT WAS NOT AT ALL POLITE!

AND HERE I THOUGHT YOU WERE A NICE BIT OF PASTRY!

HEY! FREAKSHOW...

WAS I NOT *CLEAR* ENOUGH?

I SAID--

--GET THE HELL *OFF.*

THAT GIRL?

SHE'S *OFF-LIMITS.*

Holy crap.

I've been mad before. I've lost control.

But I could have *killed* that thing.

WELL. SOMEONE'S IN A PROPER MOOD.

Um... ARE YOU OKAY?

I'M FINE, THANK YOU.

FEELING KIND OF FRISKY, TO BE HONEST WITH YOU.

NICE TO MEET YOU, BY THE WAY.

MY NAME IS RAGDOLL.

CHARMED, I'M SURE.

GAH!

It's like constricting bands of iron.

OOfff

WHAM

I can't...none of my moves *work* on him.

I MUST SAY, ALL IN ALL? THIS IS A TERRIBLE FIRST DATE.

Okay. No holds, bars, or throws. Forget about leverage.

UNGH!

Just go for tactical strikes.

How does that feel, Bendy?

UNFF--

--ENOUGH.

I SUPPOSE THIS IS WHAT I GET FOR TRYING TO DO A GOOD THING, FOR ONCE.

UNSELFISHNESS IS CLEARLY A FOOL'S PHILOSOPHY!

WHAT? "A GOOD THING"? YOU MURDERED TWO PEOPLE!

NO, I DIDN'T. I ONLY MOSTLY MURDERED THEM. THEY'LL BE FINE.

THE FULL RIDE COSTS EXTRA. I CALL IT A "HAPPY ENDING."

AND TO BE FAIR, THEY ARE TERRORISTS.

SEE? SHE'S WAKING UP.

BUT...

...ALL WE WERE GOING TO DO WAS DROP A STINK BOMB...

OH, MY, NO.

THAT STINK BOMB IS ACTUALLY A DEADLY NERVE TOXIN. IT WOULD HAVE KILLED EVERYONE IN THE BUILDING.

INCLUDING YOU DELIGHTFUL SCAMPS!

THEY HAD SOME INSIDE INFORMATION, AND I WAS THE ONLY ONE DISTURBED ENOUGH TO TAKE THIS PARTICULAR JOB.

WHAT?

I'M AFRAID YOU'VE BEEN PLAYED.

THE BATSY AND THE PATSY.

TELL YOU WHAT...

...YOU TAKE YOUR FRIENDS AND GO.

OR, YOU CAN STAY...

...AND I GIVE YOU ALL THE HAPPIEST OF ENDINGS.

NO CHARGE.

BATGIRL, I...I DIDN'T KNOW. I'M SORRY.

DON'T TRY TO TALK...JUST HANG ON TO ME.

She's slurring her words...concussion, most likely.

Gotta get her out of here.

But the key thing is someone messed with my roomie.

And that someone is going to pay.

IT WAS A NO-GO, CHARISE. THE TOXIN DIDN'T GET RELEASED.

NO MATTER. *MR. RAIN* HAS BEEN WARNED TO KEEP HIS FILTH OUT OF GOTHAM, AND THAT WAS THE *REAL* OBJECTIVE, MICHAEL.

RAIN KNEW WE WERE COMING...HE HIRED A *META*.

YES. WE HAVE A MOLE.

A *TRAITOR* IN OUR MIDST.

I UNDER-STAND, MR. RAIN.

WE'LL CLEAN UP THE SCENE, THE POLICE AND THE PAPERS WON'T HEAR A WORD.

THANK YOU, SIR.

BEDROOM OF MR. TRAVERS, A KNOWN RAIN ASSOCIATE, LATER...

MR. TRAVERS. REMEMBER ME? YOU HIRED ME.

BUT YOU WEREN'T *COMPLETELY* HONEST WITH ME, WERE YOU, YOU NAUGHTY SNOWFLAKE?

YOU DIDN'T TELL ME YOU WERE MEAN TO MONKEYS!

CONSIDER THIS MY NOTICE, SIR.

I CALL IT A HAPPY ENDING.

I RATHER LIKE MONKEYS, AS IT HAPPENS.

And Charise?

You helped me out with that weirdo, Silver.

But it doesn't mean we're on the same side.

So don't say I didn't warn you.

Too mad to think straight.

Should have prioritized those high-tech guns.

Uh oh.

Runner.

Can't have that.

They haven't said a word, even when losing *teeth.*

And they're deliberately avoiding hitting innocents.

These guys are *pros.*

Costly pros.

My experience with Gotham cops hasn't been great lately.

THERE'S A LAST ONE RABBITING, WOULD YOU MIND...?

WE'RE NOT HERE TO CLEAN UP YOUR MESSES ANYMORE.

DIDN'T YOU HEAR?

NEW *COMMISSIONER* DOESN'T LIKE YOUR *KIND.*

I'll find the guns, Charise.

Better believe that...

GOTHAM ROYAL THEATER

Hmm. I've missed the ballet again.

The price of caring about my own good work, I suppose.

Shall I call the theater, Charise? Ask the cast to go again?

No. The moment's passed, Sally.

You know, there's never been a ballet worth a damn that didn't have a broken heart in it.

I wonder if we're going to miss Gotham the way it used to be.

Doubtful.

Bit of bad news. One of our raiding parties was stopped by a vigilante in the Barcelona district.

How compromised are we?

Not too bad, I shouldn't think.

I sent Gretel to handle the snitch. The rest will get the message.

Not good enough, Sally.

Nomad protocols. You know the drill.

Who was the vigilante, may I ask?

WHO ELSE? BATGIRL.

Ha!

SOMETHING STRIKE YOU AS AMUSING?

I WAS JUST THINKING I MISSED *TWO* BALLETS TONIGHT.

TURN ON THE NEWS, WOULD YOU, SALLY?

...WORD OF A *LAWSUIT* BROUGHT AGAINST FORMER COMMISSIONER *JIM GORDON* AND THE GOTHAM CITY POLICE DEPARTMENT IN THE ALLEGEDLY WRONGFUL SHOOTING OF ONE *RICKY GUTIERREZ*...

...IN A *NOTORIOUSLY* BOTCHED *POLICE* RAID JUST TEN DAYS AGO.

NOW THIS.

THIS *INFURIATES* ME.

THAT THAT...THAT COMMON CRIMINAL *SCUM* COULD SUE A GOOD MAN LIKE JAMES *GORDON* LIKE THAT!

CHARISE, YOU *DID* ORDER THAT HONEST POLICEMAN *KILLED*, REMEMBER?

HE'S ALSO IN *JAIL* FOR *MANSLAUGHTER* OF HUNDREDS OF PEOPLE, I HATE TO POINT OUT.

THAT IS *BESIDE* THE POINT.

NO. I AM NOT HAVING THIS IN MY CITY.

I WANT YOU TO GO *VISIT* THIS MISTER GUTIERREZ, SALLY.

TONIGHT.

YES, KNIGHTFALL. MY *PLEASURE.*

She does this to me, every time.

As soon as one of her goons starts to tattle...

...Knightfall moves everyone and everything.

She has the money to rebuild, and the man-power to make it fly.

And there's only one *Batgirl*, dang it.

I got to her *once* at her fortress...she won't let that happen again.

And that's why, Barbara Gordon, for all your training, and your gear, and your smarts...

...she's always going to *beat* you.

OH.

OH!

OH, MY GOD! I'M SORRY!

SORRY SORRY SORRY!

I'M SORRY!

OH, MAN.

WE HAVE TO WORK OUT A *SIGNAL* WHEN A DATE IS OVER.

NOT THAT I EVER *HAVE* A DATE OVER...

...LIKE MAYBE A SOCK ON THE DOORKNOB, OR SOMETHING--?

HI, I'M JO, AND I SHOULD BE GOING OH, *WOW,* LOOK AT THE TIME NICE TO MEET YOU, SORRY, GOODBYE, GOODBYE!

Uh. WE WERE PLAYING SCRABBLE.

SO I GATHERED.

THAT WAS JO.

FROM THE BACK OF HER HEAD, SHE SEEMED REALLY NICE.

WE'RE KIND OF DATING.

YA THINK?

YOU KNOW, RICKY CALLED LIKE FORTY-ELEVEN TIMES.

ARE YOU GOING TO ANSWER HIM?

HE'S SUING MY *DAD,* ALYSIA.

KINDA HARD TO GET *PAST* THAT, SOMEHOW.

UPTOWN GIRL—
NO ANSWER.

DAMMIT, BARBARA... ANSWER THE *PHONE*.

MAYBE SOMEONE DOESN'T WAN' TO TALK TO YOU.

YOU... *YOU*.

HI, RICKY. REMEMBER ME? I'M THE ONE WHO AMPUTATED YOUR *LEG*, IF THAT HELPS RING A BELL.

WELL SAID. LISTEN, RICKY. IT'S LIKE THIS...

...KNIGHTFALL DOESN'T WANT A CHEAP CAR THIEF LIKE *YOU* BRINGING DOWN GOTHAM P.D. SHE THINKS IT'S BAD *FORM* TO KICK A MAN WHILE HE'S DOWN.

SO DROP THE LAWSUIT AGAINST JIM GORDON, AND I RETREAT TO YOUR NIGHTMARES. FAIR?

OR WHAT, YOU'LL TAKE THE OTHER LEG?

NO.

THAT WOULD BE *MEAN*.

YOU HAVE UNTIL TOMORROW MORNING FOR A PRESS CONFERENCE.

BREAK A LEG, RICKY.

EARLY.

I HATE YOU, EARLY.

I keep thinking about those guns, those high-tech hand-cannons.

In residential and commercial neighborhoods.

Crowds. Kids.

I have to think. I need a clear head.

Knightfall has an army. And there's just *one* Batgirl.

FOLLOW HER.

WAIT 'TIL SHE'S ISOLATED.

MS. GORDON?

YOU NEED TO COME WITH *ME*, PLEASE.

WHAT?

MUNIRA KHAIRUDDIN? *MUNI?*

I...*Uh,* HAVE A CODE NAME NOW.

IT'S *OBSCURA.*

It's... impossible...

HOW... ...HOW *COULD* YOU?

ENOUGH.

NO.

I'M JUST GETTING *STARTED*.

ALL RIGHT. FUN'S OVER.

SETTLE, BABS.

"BABS"?

>Gghh<

YOU DON'T GET TO CALL ME THAT!

Fifteen.

Both just...

...fifteeen. Too young for university.

We both went anyway.

Fought...

...all the time.

CLASS IS OVER, LADIES.

BREAK.

For us...

...class was never over...

...fought all the time.

And then I loved her.

And then she was my sister.

And then she went *away*.

I APOLOGIZE FOR ALL OF THIS, BARBARA. YOU COMING 'ROUND?

I COULDN'T TAKE THE CHANCE OF YOU RUNNING BEFORE WE HAD A CHAT.

She chose this place for a reason.

Dad told me the bad cops, they used to take guys out here to beat a *confession* out of them.

Sometimes a boa just got...*lost.*

I'm not scared, Muni. I'm just pissed *off.*

YOU WERE *DEAD.*

NO, BABS.

I WAS *RECRUITED.*

YOU WANT SOME WATER? THE SERUM MAKES YOU THIRSTY, I'VE HEARD.

IF YOU'RE THINKING OF GOING FOR MY GUN...

...THOSE AGENTS WILL SHOOT BEFORE IT CLEARS LEATHER, BARBARA.

I WAS *RECRUITED,* AGE EIGHTEEN, RIGHT OFF CAMPUS, FOR AN EYES-ONLY ELITE COUNTER-TERRORISM SQUAD, BARBARA.

THE UPSIDE WAS, I COULD END UP *LITERALLY* SAVING MY COUNTRY.

So they cover my head and drop me off basically nowhere.

THANKS *EVER* SO MUCH, GUYS.

BZZT

It's Ricky. Better face up to it.

BARBARA. IT'S OVER. TELL YOUR FATHER, OKAY? TELL HIM...TELL HIM I'M DROPPING MY LAWSUIT. EVERYTHING.

THEY HAD PEOPLE, PEOPLE IN *BLACKGATE* WITH HIM. MY *BROTHER.*

RICKY? RICKY, WHAT'S *HAPPENED?*

MY BROTHER *ROLO.*

KNIGHTFALL CUT OFF MY BROTHER'S *HAND...*

And that's when the world slipped away for a while.

I remember everything. But I don't remember how...

...everything went black and red.

My therapist would have a name for this.

But I knew it was the moment the bat inside me woke up *enraged.*

So I called the one person I knew would march to Hell with me.

To fight the damn *devil*. Everything that's wrong in this city.

NICE *ENTRANCE*, RED.

And because she is who she is, she *showed*.

The one and only *Black Canary*.

I'M IN. OF COURSE I'M IN.

LISTEN, LAST TIME YOU FACED THIS WOMAN YOU NEARLY GOT STABBED TO DEATH, AND THAT WAS *WITH* BACKUP.

KNIGHTFALL AND THE DISGRACED WILL BE *READY* THIS TIME.

EVERY TIME I SHUT DOWN AN OPERATION, SHE MOVES EVERYTHING AND EVERYONE. I CAN'T...

...I CAN'T GET TRACTION. AND I CAN'T LET HER *SLIDE* ANYMORE.

IT MIGHT BE A SUICIDE RUN.

IT'S NOT THE BEST ODDS, I'LL GRANT YOU.

MAYBE I CAN HELP?

DEADLINE PART TWO: ENEMIES AND ALLIES

GAIL SIMONE writer   FERNANDO PASARIN penciller   JONATHAN GLAPION   MATT RYAN inkers   BLOND colorist   ALEX GARNER cover artist

ENOUGH.

CANARY? WHAT THE HELL?!

STOP IT. SHE'S NOT WITH THEM. CAN'T YOU SEE THAT?

Ugnn.

YOU DON'T KNOW.

HOW CAN WE KNOW THAT?

BECAUSE, MS. NORMALLY PRETTY RATIONAL, SHE IS COVERED IN WEAPONS...

...BUT SHE'S NOT FIGHTING BACK.

Damn.

did girl come girl?

That girl who strikes first, and never thinks?

OKAY. THIS IS...THIS IS *AWKWARD.*

I'M--

A DANGEROUS LUNATIC?

NO, NO. *SORRY.* I'M SORRY.

IF YOU'RE REACHING FOR ONE OF THOSE POINTY THINGS, THERE'S A STATUTE OF LIMITATIONS ON MY NOT FIGHTING *BACK.*

NOTED.

HERE...YOU GOT A LITTLE...*um.* OKAY, A *LOT* OF BLOOD THERE.

YEAH. CLUMSY *ME.*

NORMALLY, MY FRIEND HERE IS THE *THOUGHTFUL* ONE.

IT'S BEEN A ROUGH NIGHT.

YOU SAY YOU'RE NOT FROM *AROUND* HERE?

WELL. YOU COULD SAY I'M FROM OUT OF TOWN. *WAY* OUT OF TOWN.

BUT I CARE ABOUT GOTHAM. IT *MEANS* SOMETHING TO ME.

SO I DID SOME DIGGING UPON ARRIVAL, AND FOLLOWED YOU.

AND I'M PRETTY GOOD AMMO, WHEN AIMED CORRECTLY.

I'VE NEVER HEARD OF YOU.

YOU SAYING YOU CAN REMEMBER *EVERYONE* WHO EVER--

YES.

ALL RIGHT. HERE'S THE DEAL. YOU TELL ME WHO YOU *ARE* AND YOU CAN JOIN US. OTHERWISE, NO DEAL.

REALLY? YOU SHOW ME YOURS, AND I'LL SHOW YOU *MINE*?

BATGIRL, YOU *WALED* ON HER WITH EVERYTHING YOU HAD, AND YOU COULDN'T PUT HER *DOWN*.

I, FOR ONE, WOULD LIKE TO HAVE HER STANDING UP FOR *OUR* TEAM.

I VOTE SHE GETS A SHOT.

That's Canary. She wants to give everyone a chance.

Including me, a bunch of times.

OKAY. BUT YOU EVEN *THINK* OF BETRAYING US, "HUNTRESS"...

...I WILL FIND A *WAY*, CLEAR?

AS TOAST. WANT YOUR DAINTY TOWELETTE BACK?

KEEP IT.

I DON'T KNOW HOW MUCH YOU KNOW, STRANGE LADY.

BUT HERE'S WHY WE'RE BASICALLY *SCREWED*.

"EVERY TIME WE TAKE DOWN A CELL OF KNIGHTFALL'S, NO MATTER HOW SMALL...

"...SHE MOVES *EVERYONE* ELSE.

"NO INFORMANT EVER HAS ANYTHING THAT ISN'T *OBSOLETE*.

"SHE CALLS IT THE *NOMAD PROTOCOL*."

BUT SHE'S GOT LIEUTENANTS. PEOPLE SHE TRUSTS.

META-HUMANS SHE CALLS THE *DISGRACED.*

OKAY.

AND YOU HAVE A BEAD ON ONE OF THESE EXPLOITABLE ASSETS?

BARBARA'S APARTMENT. **LATER...**

"I DO.

"BUT IT KIND OF *SUCKS* TO HAVE TO *USE* IT."

My fists actually ache from belting the purple lady.

And I thought I had a thick skull.

ROOMIE? ALYSIA?

WHAT?

IT'S FOUR IN THE...ARE YOU *OKAY*, GORDON?

KINDA. BUT I BROUGHT LEMON GINGER BISCOTTI.

YOU ARE *DEFINITELY* YOUR MOM'S DAUGHTER.

COME IN, I'LL SCOOCH OVER.

JO SEEMS NICE.

YEAH, I LIKE HER.

YOUR *DAD* CALLED. FROM... WELL, FROM *PRISON.*

SAID IT WAS IMPORTANT. SAID IT WAS A *FAMILY* MATTER.

Stay focused, Barbara. One crisis at a time.

I'M SORRY, ALYSIA. BUT I NEED TO KNOW WHO HOOKED YOU TWO INTO SABOTAGING THAT BUILDING LAST WEEK.

I CAN'T TELL YOU WHY.

Hmf. YOU THINK I DON'T *KNOW* WHY?

YOU THINK I DON'T KNOW WHO YOU *REALLY* ARE, GORDON?

YOU WATCH THOSE CRIME SHOWS ALL DAY, YOU COME HOME BEAT UP, THUGS COME TO OUR HOUSE *LOOKING* FOR YOU.

YOU THINK I CAN'T CONNECT THOSE DOTS?

Uh, oh.

YOU'RE AN *UNDERCOVER COP*, RIGHT?

YOU WORK FOR YOUR *DAD*, SOMEHOW.

Oh, thank God.

ONLY, WITH THE TROUBLE WITH YOUR DAD, I FIGURED YOU'D BE OFF-DUTY?

ESPECIALLY WHERE TRESPASSING ROOMMATES ARE INVOLVED?

OKAY.

IT'S *SOMETHING* LIKE THAT.

I know it's wrong. Keeping secrets from the best friend I've ever had.

But I can't pull her any deeper into this. I can't.

ALYSIA, SOMETHING BAD IS HAPPENING. SOMETHING THAT'S GOING TO TAKE OUR NEIGHBORHOOD AND BURN IT *DOWN.*

WHO TRIED TO TALK YOU INTO PLANTING THAT BOMB?

THE THREE TOWERS...

"MICHAEL.

"HIS NAME WAS *MICHAEL.*"

I WARNED THEM A GERM ATTACK WOULD COME SOMEDAY.

THEY DIDN'T *LISTEN.*

SO YOU TOOK YOUR TOXIC ABILITIES TO YOUR HIGH SCHOOL.

TO MAKE THEM *UNDERSTAND* THE *DANGER*.

WELL.

THAT WAS *THEN*, MICHAEL.

AMERICA HAS ENEMIES. *GOTHAM* HAS ENEMIES.

THEY NEED TO BE PREPARED. THAT'S WHY I'M HERE, KNIGHTFALL.

WITH YOU.

LET'S CALL A GAS ATTACK ON THE POPULATION A BIT OF A *LAST RESORT*, SHALL WE?

IF THEY DON'T MEET MY DEADLINE, PLEASE, FEEL *FREE*.

GO GET SOME REST, MICHAEL. BIG, BIG DAY TOMORROW.

THINK HE'S UP FOR THE DEADLINE?

HE WANTS WHAT WE WANT: WHAT'S *BEST* FOR GOTHAM.

HE WANTS THE BAD PEOPLE DEAD OR GONE. *ALL* OF THEM.

IN THE NEXT SIXTEEN HOURS, HE GETS HIS *WISH*.

DID YOU CALL THE OPERATIVES AS REQUESTED, *BONEBREAKER*?

OH, YES, KNIGHTFALL.

WE CALLED *EVERYONE*.

THREE TOWERS PARKING GARAGE...

WE HAVE A NINETY-SECOND WINDOW BEFORE SECURITY COMES TO CHECK THE CAMERA BLACKOUT.

WATCH HIS HANDS.

HE'S A WALKING *CHEMICAL SPILL*, GOT IT.

WATCH HIS *HANDS*, HUNTRESS.

HEY. BUDDY-ROO.

LOOKING FOR A GOOD TIME?

YES. OH, VERY *MUCH* SO.

GUESS THE TEMPORARY TRUCE IS *OVER*, YES?

Tssssss

Um. THANKS?

DON'T *MENTION* IT.

Her weapons were for show, to get a surrender.

We can't risk a concussion, or shattered eardrums, or worse.

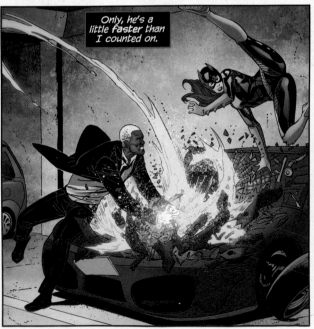

Only, he's a little *faster* than I counted on.

And a *hell* of a lot more *powerful*.

She didn't...she didn't say she could *fly.*

Can she actually *fly?!*

WELL, THAT'S THIS ONE OUT AND DOWN. GO, *TEAM.*

THAT WAS *INCREDIBLY* RECKLESS.

HE COULD HAVE *MELTED* YOU.

NO CHOICE, THOUGH.

WHAT? WHY NOT?

DON'T YOU KNOW?

HE WAS MESSING WITH MY *PARTNER.*

HEY, uh... GUYS? WE HAVE A *WITNESS.*

WITNESS? WHAT WITNESS?

I WAS JUST GOIN' TO GET MY *RIDE.*

OKAY, WE'RE GHOSTS. WE ARE *PAST* THE NINETY-SECOND MARK.

YEAH. OKAY.

GONE. WE'RE *GONE.*

DO YOURSELF A FAVOR AND GET *OUT* OF THE AREA, LADY!

MOTHER MARY *MAYDAY.*

This went messier than we planned for.

They'll see the car. They'll know he was taken.

No hiding it now.

We're all in.

HEY. HEY, MICHAEL *DRUCKER.*

BLEAK MICHAEL, THEY CALL YOU, RIGHT?

MAYBE YOU'RE THINKING OF FIRING UP THAT *ACID* GOOP...

...I WOULDN'T.

I MEAN, IT'S YOUR CALL.

BUT *ME*, I'D THINK IT OVER.

CHARISE. IT'S *MICHAEL*. THEY'VE *GOT* HIM.

STUPID MAN. ALL RIGHT.

PREPARE FOR OUR DEPARTURE. WE'LL RUN OPERATIONS FROM THE *THEMIS*.

AND *BONEBREAKER*...

"...SEND A SQUAD AND *FIND* HIM."

YOU THINK I'M AFRAID OF DEATH?

TO SAVE MY CITY, I AM *PREPARED* TO DIE.

MICHAEL. I READ YOUR *FILE*.

YOU WERE A CHILD PRODIGY, A GENIUS WITH CHEMICALS.

AND I DO BELIEVE YOU WANT TO *HELP* GOTHAM.

PLEASE, MICHAEL. WE KNOW KNIGHTFALL HAS A PLAN, AND WE KNOW IT'S BAD. HELP US.

YOU *CAN* BE THE HERO, HERE.

I CAN GET THE INFORMATION, JUST LET ME--

NO, WAIT. SHE'S GOOD AT THIS. LET HER TRY.

HELP US, MICHAEL. HELP US SAVE GOTHAM.

I... I CAN'T. I *CAN'T.*

TARGETS *ACQUIRED,* COMMAND.

THE ORDER IS *GIVEN,* GENTLE-MEN.

Dammit.

We took too long.

WELL. WHAT THE *HELL,* RIGHT?

THE SHIELDS ARE *ATTACKING,* REPEAT, WE ARE *UNDER ATTACK.*

PLEASE *ADVISE.*

Let's go be a hurricane.

Guh. HANG **ON**.

I COULD... I COULD *BURN* YOU RIGHT NOW.

THEN I *BURN*.

HANG **ON**.

OKAY. OKAY, BATGIRL. WE GOT HIM.

THANK GOD.

SHE'S GOT A DEADLINE. *MIDNIGHT TONIGHT...* FIFTEEN AND A HALF HOURS.

EVERY CRIMINAL LEAVES CHERRY HILL.

OR THEY *DIE*.

THAT...THAT'S *IMPOSSIBLE*.

OH, IT'S *VERY* POSSIBLE. IT'S ALREADY IN *MOTION*.

SHE'S HIRED MERCS FROM ALL OVER THE *WORLD*. IT'S AN *ARMY*.

WE'LL STOP HER. WE'LL STORM THE *BUILDING*.

KNIGHTFALL'S NOT IN GOTHAM ANYMORE. NOT EXACTLY.

IT'S OVER.

YOU ALL SHOULD JUST LEAVE, WHILE YOU *CAN*.

SO...I DON'T KNOW WHAT WE DO HERE.

IF WE ATTACK ONE HEAD, SHE MOVES THE ENTIRE BODY. THAT'S HER M.O., RIGHT?

THERE JUST AREN'T ENOUGH WARM *BODIES* ON OUR SIDE.

NOT. YET. BUT I HAVE SOME CALLS TO MAKE.

DETECTIVE McKENNA. IT'S BATGIRL.

I NEED YOU TO LISTEN *VERY* CAREFULLY.

I'M LISTENING, GOTHAM. MAKE IT *GOOD*.

WAIT. SAY THAT AGAIN. *WHAT* ARE YOU OFFERING ME, BARBARA?

YOU HEARD ME. YOU WANT ME TO *WORK* FOR YOU, THIS IS HOW IT HAPPENS, MUNI.

AND IN RETURN?

YOU HAVE CONTACT INFO FOR *EVERYONE*, RIGHT?

THAT'S WHO WE NEED. TONIGHT. *EVERYONE*.

I NEED AN HOUR WITH YOUR *CONTACT LIST*, MUNIRA KHAIRUDDIN. FOR A *FRIEND*.

WE'RE IN.

THIS *LAST* ONE'S GONNA BE A *TOUGHIE*...

"WE'VE BROUGHT IN VETTED MERCS FROM *EVERYWHERE.*

YOU THINK SO? WE'VE BEEN PLANNING FOR THIS FOR *YEARS,* BATGIRL.

WE'VE SPENT *MILLIONS.*

"WE WILL ACCOMPLISH IN *ONE NIGHT* WHAT YOU PEOPLE HAVEN'T EVEN MADE A DENT AGAINST IN *YEARS.*

"EVERY PETTY *DEALER,* EVERY *FLESH PEDDLER,* EVERY *CRIMINAL LEFT* WILL BE *DONE.*

"ONE *PROBLEM,* ONE *BULLET.*

"WE *WARNED* THEM, BATGIRL. THEY COULD HAVE *LEFT.*

"NOW, THEY ARE *VERMIN.*"

YEAH.

ONLY, SEE, THE THING IS?

I CALLED IN A FEW PEOPLE *MYSELF.*

GUH.

YOU COME *AT* ME, LITTLE *SMARTASS*?

TELL YOU WHAT.

I WAS *GONNA* LET YOUR MAMA *GO*.

GUESS WE CAN FORGET ABOUT *THAT* NOW, CAN'T WE?

NO. *NO!*

GGHH.

LIEUTENANT MELODY McKENNA, G.C.P.D.

YOU MIGHT REMEMBER KNOCKING ME COLD ON YOUR FIRE ESCAPE?

I'M HERE TO GET YOU *OUT*.

SOMEONE PRETTY HIGH *UP* WANTS YOU PROTECTED *BAD*.

AND I OWE HER A *FAVOR*. BUT I WARN YOU BOTH...

I would say some *payback* is due, here.

GHHHUHK

WAS GONNA... ...BE *PRINCESS*.

OKAY. BE SLEEPING *BEAUTY*, THEN.

COPS, BATGIRL?

YOU SEND *COPS* AGAINST MY ARMY?

IT WON'T *WORK*. IT WON'T *BEGIN* TO STOP THEM.

"I HIRED *METAHUMANS*, BATGIRL."

"ALL YOU'VE DONE IS MAKE SURE THE *POLICE* DIE IN THE SAME GUTTERS AS THE CRIMINAL *FILTH*."

YOU KNOW THE DRILL, EVERYONE.

CUT OFF THE *HANDS* TO COLLECT THE *BOUNTY*.

NO *PROOF*, NO *PAY*.

A MOST *SOUND* STRATEGY, *INDEED.*

I knew Agent Obscura would keep her word. She was my roommate once, she never broke a promise ever.

And I had asked for an hour alone with her Rolodex.

WHAT... WHAT THE HELL IS *HAPPENNING?*

HEY, NOW, DON'T YOU COME ANY *CLOSER*, BEAUTIFUL.

IT DOESN'T MATTER. I'LL MOVE MY OPERATIONS, YOU WON'T KNOW WHERE TO *LOOK*, WHERE THEY'LL *STRIKE!*

OH, RIGHT. THAT'S YOUR S.O.P. WHEN ONE OF YOUR CELLS IS TAKEN DOWN. "OPERATION: NOMAD," RIGHT? MOVE *EVERYONE*.

HOW...HOW COULD YOU *KNOW* ABOUT THAT?

BECAUSE I *TOLD* YOU. LAST TIME WE *FOUGHT*, REMEMBER?

You said you own the servers and the data-bases.

THEN I'LL LEARN TO BEAT THOSE, *TOO*.

YOU...YOU CRACKED *MY* SYSTEM?

THAT'S *IMPOSSIBLE*.

NO, NOT AT ALL. SEE... COMPUTERS?

IT TURNS OUT I'M FREAKING *GOOD* AT THOSE.

SO WE HAD A *PLAN* FOR YOUR NOMAD CONTINGENCY, CHARISE.

ATTACKING *ONE* CELL ONLY LET THE OTHERS *BOLT*, WHICH IS WHY ME, BY MYSELF...I COULD NEVER GET ANY *TRACTION*.

"BUT BETWEEN THE PEOPLE WHO OWED MY FRIEND *OBSCURA* A FAVOR...AND A FEW OF *MY* FRIENDS...

"WE COVERED *ALL* YOUR HIDEY HOLES.

"AT THE *SAME DAMN TIME*."

THESE GUYS ARE *BAD CHEESE* AND THERE'S *WAY* TOO MANY, VIRTUE!

KEEP *FIGHTING*, MOUSE. WE PROMISED *BATGIRL*!

HEY, GUYS. MIND IF I HELP OUT?

Okay. I once beat Knightfall within an inch of her life and it only made her *mad.*

Time to use the *big guns.*

HANG ON, I HAVE SOMETHING TO SHOW YOU, CHARISE.

LOOK *OUT.* SHE'S GOING FOR A *WEAPON!*

OH, SHUT *UP,* GROTESQUE. NO ONE WAS *TALKING* TO YOU.

IT'S YOUR FAMILY, CHARISE.

I DON'T KNOW ABOUT HEAVEN, OR THE AFTERLIFE.

BUT...WHAT IF THEY *ARE* WATCHING YOU?

IT'S OVER.

I PUT ALL YOUR DATA ON THE WEB. EVERYTHING YOU'VE DONE.

NOWHERE IN THE *WORLD* IS FAR ENOUGH TO HIDE.

I THOUGHT, I THOUGHT WE WOULD...

I DON'T WANT TO FIGHT YOU, CHARISE.

I DON'T THINK YOU TRULY *KNOW* WHAT YOU'VE DONE.

YOU NEED HELP.

I WANT TO BELIEVE.

I'M SO TIRED.

The cop choppers. The data went out*, I guess.*

I DON'T KNOW IF THIS'LL TAKE, BATGIRL. I REALLY DON'T.

BUT I WANT TO GIVE YOU A PRESENT. FOR THE *PHOTO.*

YOUR BROTHER?

HE'S *ALIVE.*

SO, YOU'RE NOT A *KILLER,* AFTER ALL.

The cops mumbled something as they took her away.

It didn't connect.

BATGIRL...YOU SAVED GOD *KNOWS* HOW MANY LIVES.

SOMETIMES A WIN--IT STILL FEELS LIKE A LOSS, YOU KNOW?

The thing is...I believe Charise.

I'm not a murderer.

And that changes everything.

SHUT UP AND HUG, TOUGH GIRL.

And that changes everything.

YES!

Because if I'm not James' killer...

...then I still have a chance to be the Barbara I *want* to be. Starting *tonight*, everything *changes*.

OW.

Also, everything hurts.

Fingers are so swollen I can barely work the door.

Sleeping out front with the bat in hand.

She must've been *terrified*.

GOTHAM UNDER SIEGE

ALYSIA?

GORDON?

THANK *GOD*.

I WAS *WORRIED*. IF YOU DIDN'T SHOW UP, I WAS GOING TO GO LOOKING FOR YOU.

LOOKING FOR ME? IN THAT WAR ZONE OUTSIDE?

She would have done it, too. I know she would have.

And I make a decision.

She stuck by me through the Joker, through my brother.

She treated me like a sister.

HANG ON A SECOND, ALYSIA. *UH*...

...THIS IS GOING TO BE WEIRD.

IT'S TIME. IT'S TIME FOR ME TO GO. TO LEAVE HERE AND START *OVER*.

WHAT?

WHAT DO YOU *MEAN*?

GAIL SIMONE writer JAVIER GARRÓN artist ROMULO FAJARDO, JR. colorist
CLAY MANN & ROMULO FAJARDO, JR. cover artists

"NO. IF HE SEES YOU, HE'LL KILL YOU."

"BUT BEAST, WE CAN *TAKE* HIM."

"NO. COME BACK *NOW*, OR YOU'RE *OUT*."

After the wedding... I did nothing, for six months.

Except hunt *data*.

And what the net couldn't tell me, I found out for *myself*.

I became the inside man.

I worked as a gun moll, as a henchman, for all the *baddest* in the *boy band*.

Batman's excellent with disguises.

Guess who...?

Greetings from the Iceberg Lounge xoxo

But not *that* excellent.

In a way, it's almost quaint. They never saw me as a threat, never noticed me at all.

Two years it took me, underground, to dismantle 70% of the crime syndicates in Gotham.

Until my *hand* was on their *throat*.

Barbara Gordon was gone from the map *forever*.

And I learned awful knowledge from each of those brilliant minds. Until there was only one left to confront.

BANE.
I
AM *NO ONE*.
I COME FROM
NOWHERE.

TEACH ME.

AH. THEN YOU MUST WALK IN MY FOOTSTEPS, DAUGHTER.

BUT YOU WILL NEVER AGAIN BE THAT CHILD ON MY DOORSTEP.

And I...became the Black Beast. *Bête Noire*.

I had a chance to kill him, but I couldn't do it.

And so I walked out.

And he was right.

I was never a child *again*.

BLACK BEAST. MY *RED-TRESSED* DAUGHTER.

It's him. He's in my system.

Always ten times *smarter* than anyone knows.

I AM WATCHING YOUR THREE CHARGES, DAUGHTER.

THE *QUIET* ONE SEEMS *PARTICULARLY* DANGEROUS.

I HAVE IN MY HANDS A DETONATOR, CONNECTED TO SIX BOMBS IN CROWDED AREAS. YOU WILL NOT FIND THEM IN TIME.

I FEEL YOU SHOULD COME SETTLE THIS BETWEEN US. YOU *SHAMED* AND *DECEIVED* ME...

...AFTER MY *VENOM* MADE YOU A *GODDESS*.

COME FINISH YOUR *TRAINING*, ONCE AND FOR ALL.

FINE. I'M COMING.

VARIANT COVER GALLERY

BATGIRL 27
Scribblenauts variant cover by Jon Katz after Carmine Infantino

BATGIRL 28
Steampunk variant cover by J.G. Jones and Trish Mulvihill

BATGIRL 29
Robot Chicken variant cover by Adam Hughes and RC Stoodios

BATGIRL 30
MAD variant cover by Rick Tulka and Carl Peterson

BATGIRL 31
BATMAN '66 variant cover by Mike and Laura Allred

BATGIRL 32
DC Bombshell variant cover by Ant Lucia

BATGIRL 33
Batman 75th anniversary variant cover by Cliff Chiang and Mike Kaluta

BATGIRL 34
Selfie variant cover by Dave Johnson

Greetings From

GOTHAM
CITY

Cover sketches by Alex Garner for BATGIRL #29, 31 &33

BATGIRL #30 cover pencils by Clay Mann